The Gospels in Harmony

Bible readings and original poems
that reveal the life of Jesus

Martin Wild

Onwards and Upwards Publishers

3 Radfords Turf
Cranbrook
Exeter
EX5 7DX
United Kingdom

www.onwardsandupwards.org

First edition, published in the United Kingdom by Onwards and Upwards Publishers (2018).

ISBN: 978-1-78815-737-7
Cover design: LM Graphic Design

Printed in the United Kingdom.

About the Author

Martin has lived for the past thirty years in a village in Staffordshire with his wife Sue. They have been married for nearly fifty years and have two married daughters and six grandchildren.

Martin worked for much of his career for a multinational brewing and hospitality company working in such diverse areas as IT, electronic gaming and branded restaurants. On his retirement he helped to establish a software company in the housebuilding industry as well as working as a freelance IT consultant.

Martin is part of the leadership team of Tamworth Elim Church where he has worshipped for the past twenty years since coming to faith. He is also the leader of a small band of Christian storytellers organising many events over the years including the telling of the Gospels of Mark and John and modern interpretations of the parables.

Martin's previous book, *Twice Times Telling – The Books of the Bible in Poetry,* was originally published in 2011 and republished in paperback and eBook format with the title *Start to Finish* in early 2017.

Endorsement

A valuable tool for personal or group devotion or study of the life of Christ, to be used throughout the Christian year, but of special help for the growing practice of contemplative prayer where the often vividly expressed and thought-provoking insights of these poems come to life. I shall be widely recommending this ambitious series of poems.

Dr Richard Massey
Former Principal
Birmingham Bible Institute / Birmingham Christian College.

Acknowledgements

Thanks...

To God my Creator and Saviour
who has pursued me with his love
and in whom I have found life itself.

To my late parents
who raised me in the knowledge of Jesus Christ.

To all of my fellow believers and workers
in the Elim Church in Tamworth, England,
as we have lived and worked alongside each other
and through whose example I have come to understand
both the challenges and the fullness of the Christian life.

To the translators and publishers of the NIV version of the Bible
whose work inspired this poetry.

Dedication

To my wife Sue and all my immediate family
who are all deeply precious to me:

my daughters Elizabeth and Katherine;
my sons-in-law Tim and Jamie;
my grandchildren Ethan, Jude, Jessica, Josiah, Zachary and Elijah;

and

to my pastor Steve, and his wife Julie,
whose wisdom has informed my faith
and whose friendship has enriched my life.

The true goal of music – its proper enterprise – is melody.

All the parts of harmony have as their ultimate purpose a single beautiful melody.

Johann Philipp Kirnberger (1771)

Contents

Ministry (continued)

Ministry (continued)

Passion, Death and Resurrection 109

The Gospels 135

Preface

I was brought up in a large Catholic family in England, attending schools in Yorkshire, Hampshire and Shropshire as work moved us around the country. Sunday church was always a part of the fabric of life and like many boys of my age and time, I attended Bible study classes and served at church services, firstly in stumbling Latin and later in English. Scripture was part of the warp and weft of life though, couched in liturgy and ceremony, increasingly removed from the post war society that was gathering pace around it.

Over the subsequent thirty years, I veered between times of regular church attendance and indifference, at times assuaging my uncertainties by ensuring that my daughters were brought up in the Catholic tradition until they were old enough to choose for themselves.

At the age of 48, through a sequence of events within my family, I came to visit the Tamworth Elim Church. On that very first Sunday in 1997, I became aware in a profound and life-changing way that the love and grace of God was the foundation of Christian faith; after a few weeks of heartfelt searching and prayer, I accepted Christ into my life.

Shortly afterwards, on a business trip to the USA, I had time to visit a Christian bookstore in Atlanta. I found myself standing somewhat awestruck in front of shelves of Bibles, uncertain of how to choose one to buy. I was grateful for the guidance given by the nameless shop assistant who guided me to my NIV Study Bible, the well-thumbed pages of which are deeply treasured to this day.

Reading the scriptures for myself was like awakening to a new world of exploration and awareness, and I rapidly became immersed in study and discussion. So much of what I had learnt by rote as a child now came to make true sense for the very first time.

All of my life I have loved poetry and my favourite author since my teenage years has been Gerard Manley Hopkins. His profound spirituality combined with his unique gift of dense yet spare imagery has remained with me. In 2010, the concept of a poetic anthology of the Bible came to me – with one poem for each and every book of the Old and New Testaments. *Twice Times Telling* was published in 2011 – its title referencing the name of Deuteronomy, which means a 'second telling of the law'. The volume contains not only poems for each book of scripture but complementary word clouds using words from the texts themselves. The book was re-published in 2017 under the title *Start to Finish* in both paperback and eBook format.

In 2016, the urge to write a more in-depth collection of poems for the Gospels was born, together with the notion of linking all four Gospels together into a single poetic narrative. This is *The Gospels in Harmony*. My hope and prayer is that this new volume will draw you into a deeper study and reflection on scripture and, in so doing, enrich your faith and trust in the saving grace of God through Christ his Son.

Foreword by Rev. Dr Steve Jonathan

Martin Wild, an extraordinary man – husband, father, grandfather, businessman, storyteller, church leader, counsellor, teacher, poet, historian, follower of Jesus and, I'm privileged to say, friend. In 1997, Martin walked into Tamworth Elim Church in the English Midlands, having looked for a Pentecostal Church, at his daughter's request, in the Yellow Pages. This was a world before Google.

Martin was instantly gripped by God's grace and continued attending, most weeks in tears, as he began experiencing that same grace through contemporary worship songs, Bible teaching and Christian love. These visits were supplemented with coffee and cakes in my office as Martin sought answers to his questions. He discovered the answers he coveted, but received more, much more: he also experienced God's peace, forgiveness, joy in his heart, hope for the future and a totally transformed life. He has never looked back.

My fear for Martin in the early days was that he would run out of steam. He just wanted to serve Jesus in any way and every way he had opportunity. He commenced his spiritual journey at one hundred miles an hour and has kept up his passion for Jesus and his kingdom ever since. Although Martin does not have any formal theological training or an ecclesiastical ordination, my wife Julie refers to Martin as her 'pastor' and I doubt that she is alone in so doing. Martin is a man of great integrity, spirituality, compassion and amazing ability. These poems are the fruit of his walk with God for over two decades.

The Gospels in Harmony is poetry inspired by Martin's reading of the Gospel accounts in the New Testament. The poetry will take you back to the original stories and I pray that these poems will fill readers' hearts with wonder and praise, that the God who came to sit where we sit, stand where we stand and endure our pain is the God who desires to journey with us through life.

I believe that this collection will delight regular readers of poetry and others, like me, not so well acquainted with it, encouraging us to stop a little longer and reflect a little deeper on words of light and life, and then stand amazed in wonder at God's grace found supremely in the person of Jesus. This book is a wonderful gift for one's private devotion and as a resource for corporate church worship.

Rev. Dr Steve Jonathan
Senior Pastor, Tamworth Elim Church
Author of *Grace Beyond the Grave*

Poem List with Gospel Cross-references

	Poem	Matthew	Mark	Luke	John
1	Divine purpose			1:1-4	1:1-18
2	Preparations			1:5-56	
3	Birthright	1:1-25		3:23-38	
4	Prophet's voice			1:57-80	
5	Welcome			2:1-20	
6	Presentations			2:21-38	
7	Dreams	2:1-23		2:39-40	
8	Home from home			2:41-52	
9	Herald	3:1-12	1:1-8	3:1-18	1:19-28
10	Jordan's water	3:13-17	1:9-11	3:21-38	1:29-34
11	Desert's end	4:1-17	1:12-15	4:1-15	4:43-45
12	Followers	4:18-22	1:16-20	5:1-11	1:35-51
13	Capernaum's time	4:23-25; 8:14-17	1:21-39	4:31-44	
14	Cana				2:1-11
15	Nicodemus				3:1-21
16	Bridegroom's voice				3:22-36
17	Rebukes and questions			3:19-20	
18	I am he				4:1-42
19	Second sign				4:46-54
20	If	8:1-4	1:40-45	5:12-16	
21	Paralytic	9:1-8	2:1-12	5:17-26	
22	Dining with the Master	9:9-17	2:13-22	5:27-39	
23	Rule-breaker				5:1-47
24	Destiny's walk	12:1-21	2:23-3:12	6:1-11	
25	Eternity's echoes		3:13-19	6:12-16	
26	Attitudes	5:1-20		6:17-26; 11:33-36	
27	The price of heaven	5:21-48		6:27-36	
28	The Son's prayer	6:1-18		11:1-8	
29	True treasures	6:19-34		12:22-34	
30	Hillside stories	7:1-14		6:37-42; 11:9-13	

	Poem	Matthew	Mark	Luke	John
31	Foundations	7:15-29		6:43-49	
32	Greater faith	8:5-13		7:1-10	
33	Nain			7:11-17	
34	Soul lessons	11:1-30		7:18-5	
35	Disciples			8:1-3	
36	Divided houses	12:22-45	3:20-30	11:14-32	
37	Family	12:46-50	3:31-35	8:19-21	
38	Seeds	13:1-23	4:1-25	8:4-18	
39	Hidden love	13:24-52	4:26-34	13:18-21	
40	Stormy waters	8:23-27	4:35-41	8:22-25	
41	Legion	8:28-34	5:1-20	8:26-39	
42	Compassion	9:18-38	5:21-43	8:40-56	
43	Rejection	13:53-58	6:1-6	4:16-30	
44	The twelve	10:1-42	6:7-13	9:1-6	
45	The Son	14:1-36	6:14-56	9:7-17	6:1-21
46	Food for life				6:22-71
47	Dirty hands	15:1-20	7:1-23		
48	Soul food	15:21-39	7:24-8:10		
49	Witnesses	16:1-28	8:11-9:1	9:18-27	
50	Chosen Son	17:1-13	9:2-13	9:28-36	
51	Faith and doubt	17:14-23	9:14-32	9:37-45; 17:5-6	
52	Two drachma tax	17:24-27			
53	The greatest	18:1-14	9:33-50	9:46-50; 17:1-2	
54	Forgiveness	18:15-35		17:3-4	
55	Divine destiny	8:18-22		9:51-62	
56	Divisions				7:1-52
57	Dust				7:53-8:11
58	Old and new				8:12-59
59	God's messengers			10:1-24	
60	Samaritans			10:25-37	
61	Bethany's cares			10:38-42	
62	Blind guides			11:37-54	
63	Fear not			12:1-12	
64	Inheritance			12:13-21	
65	Future's end			12:35-13:9; 17:7-10	

	Poem	Matthew	Mark	Luke	John
66	Unbound			13:10-17	
67	Siloam's water				9:1-41
68	Gatekeeper				10:1-21
69	Dedication				10:22-42
70	The narrow door			13:22-35	
71	Exchange			14:1-24	
72	Life's journey			14:25-35	
73	Found			15:1-32	
74	True riches			16:1-31	
75	Life and death				11:1-57
76	Ten			17:11-19	
77	Coming kingdom			17:20-37	
78	Persistence			18:1-8	
79	Two prayers			18:9-14	
80	Love	19:1-12	10:1-12		
81	Carpenter's hands	19:13-15	10:13-16	18:15-17	
82	Life-giving treasure	19:16-30	10:17-31	18:18-30	
83	Equality	20:1-16			
84	Fearful mystery	20:17-19	10:32-34	18:31-34	
85	Blindness	20:20-34	10:35-52	18:35-43	
86	God's taxman			19:1-10	
87	Minas' tale			19:11-27	
88	God's heart	26:1-16	14:1-11	7:36-50; 22:1-6	12:1-11
89	Fig tree faith	21:1-22	11:1-26	19:28-48	2:12-25; 12:12-19
90	Light and dark				12:20-50
91	Stones	21:23-46	11:27-37	20:20-44	
92	Choices	22:1-14			
93	Riddles	22:15-46	12:13-57	20:20-44	
94	Tombs	23:1-39	12:38-40	20:45-47	
95	Mite		12:41-44	21:1-4	
96	End times	24:1-25	13:1-23	21:5-24	
97	The sign of Noah	24:26-51	13:24-37	21:25-38	
98	Three tales end	25:1-46			
99	Passover's end	26:17-19	14:12-16	22:7-13	
100	Servant king				13:1-20
101	Final gathering	26:20-35	14:17-31	22:14-38	13:21-38

	Poem	Matthew	Mark	Luke	John
102	Departing words				14:1-16:33
103	Valediction				17:1-26
104	Garden of sorrows	26:36-56	14:32-52	22:39-53	18:1-11
105	Denial's right	26:57-75	14:53-72	22:54-65	18:12-27
106	The innocent I AM	27:1-26	15:1-15	22:66-23:25	18:28-19:16
107	Golgotha's moment	27:27-44	15:16-32	22:26-43	19:17-27
108	Signs and silence	27:45-66	15:33-47	23:44-56	19:28-42
109	Son rise	28:1-15	16:1-11	24:1-12	20:1-18
110	New hope		16:12-13	24:13-35	
111	Doubt and faith		16:14	24:36-49	20:19-31
112	Fisher of men				21:1-14
113	Ending and beginning	28:16-20	16:15-20	24:50-53; Acts 1	

Beginnings

1

Divine purpose
Luke 1:1-4 and John 1:1-18

With this in mind, since I myself have carefully investigated everything from the beginning, I too decided to write an orderly account for you, most excellent Theophilus, so that you may know the certainty of the things you have been taught.

Luke 1:3-4

In the beginning was the Word, and the Word was with God, and the Word was God. He was with God in the beginning.

John 1:1-2

Most excellent of friends who seek
To know the very truth of God
From those who saw with their own eyes
The ground on which he trod...
When all was nought but dark and void,
No light or life or stars or space,
The voice of God spoke all things forth;
The essence of the human race.
But true to freedom's choice and curse,
The light of God was shunned
Even as he gave all life
To those he loved as sons.
So from the very birth of time
God's rescue work began
To reconcile this broken world
Through Christ the Son of Man.
These words are so that you may know
All things have come at last
According to the ancient texts
Come down from ages past.

2

Preparations
Luke 1:5-56

Once when Zechariah's division was on duty and he was serving as priest before God, he was chosen by lot, according to the custom of the priesthood, to go into the temple of the Lord and burn incense.

Luke 1:8-9

For fifteen hundred years
The line of priests extends
A sacred cord into the holiest place
Where incense burns and prayer ascends.
And there in silent gloom
At altar's hand
The angel of the Lord appeared
With words of prophecy and strict command.
Then six months' silence
Broken by an angel's word:
'Fear not, most favoured lady,'
The choice of God is heard.
Twin miracles announced,
By divine will conceived,
The desert harbinger of God's good plan
And servant king, the Son of Man.
And as their mothers' shared embrace
Unites the unborn boys,
Flow silent words through time and space
Of love, of pain and untold joys.

3

Birthright
Matthew 1:1-25

All this took place to fulfil what the Lord had said through the prophet: 'The virgin will conceive and give birth to a son, and they will call him Immanuel'...

Matthew 1:22-23

Three times fourteen generations
From Abraham to Christ
Cascades the birthright of mankind,
Two thousand years the price.
And this first coming,
Hidden in a virgin girl,
Protected by a carpenter's chopped hands
And faithful listening;
So comes the Son of Man
By prophecy foretold,
Our God with us, Immanuel,
Isaiah's name of old.
'Fear not,' God's messenger declares,
'For now is come
He who saves his children
More numerous than stars.'

See also Luke 3:23-38

4

Prophet's voice
Luke 1:57-80

His father Zechariah was filled with the Holy Spirit and prophesied...

Luke 1:67

In the hill country of Judea
On God's appointed day,
His greatest prophet and desert wanderer
Is born.
A father's tongue at last unbound
Gives voice in song of prophecy
For all the world.
This child, the greatest born of woman
And prophet of the Most High,
Will go before to prepare the way
And give his people the knowledge of salvation.
The light of heaven
Will shine on those living in darkness
And guide their feet on the path of peace.

5

Welcome

Luke 2:1-20

But Mary treasured up all these things and pondered them in her heart.

Luke 2:19

Ruler of empire –
Merest pawn in God's good hands –
Decrees that all must go, and so ordains
Fulfilling of prophetic plans.
The birthing pains of labour's love
Born in the shadow of God's holy hill
As heralds sing the coming of this child
Who will complete God's perfect will.
Keepers of sheep the first to know
The shepherd of mankind is here,
As virgin mother treasures deep
Her heartfelt wonder and her deepest fear.

6

Presentations
Luke 2:21-38

Then Simeon blessed them and said to Mary, his mother: 'This child is destined to cause the falling and rising of many in Israel, and to be a sign that will be spoken against, so that the thoughts of many hearts will be revealed. And a sword will pierce your own soul too.'

Luke 2:34-35

Eight days and forty both;
Due times ordained for temple sacrifice and celebration,
Marking the coming of the firstborn son.
Prophetic laws laid down
In desert exile eons gone.
As redeeming offering is given,
'The light of revelation to all mankind' is lifted high
With words that pierce the soul;
The child to bring men down
But also make man whole.

7

Dreams
Matthew 2:1-23

After Jesus was born in Bethlehem in Judea, during the time of King Herod, Magi from the east came to Jerusalem and asked, 'Where is the one who has been born king of the Jews?'

Matthew 2:1-2a

'King of the Jews'
Declared by mystics from afar,
Though opposed by men of power,
Foreshadows life's eventual end
And our salvation
In its finishing.
Meanwhile, God's carpenter
And earthly child's good guardian
Escapes by means
Of four night's dreams
To Egypt
And returns to Nazareth's mean streets
To wait for his announcing.
Prophet voices echo
Through the corridors of time and man
To speak of kingship, destiny
And death.
Yet all is done in line
With God's good plan.

See also Luke 2:39-40

8

Home from home
Luke 2:41-52

'Why were you searching for me?' he asked. 'Didn't you know I had to be in my Father's house?' But they did not understand what he was saying to them.

Luke 2:49-50

Pilgrimage to Passover,
Prophetic feast of rescue and redemption;
The moment for a coming of age
And unnoticed declaration.
This temple, home from home,
The centre of both wisdom and a nation's history,
Of cut and thrust where faith is sharpened;
And yet, God's plan remains the deeper mystery.
A young man's destiny is glimpsed in pillared hall,
But still the time ordained is not yet now
And, quiet, he returns to Galilee
To wait his divine call.

9

Herald
Matthew 3:1-12

In those days John the Baptist came, preaching in the wilderness of Judea and saying, 'Repent, for the kingdom of heaven has come near.'

Matthew 3:1-2

Fed with sweetened locust,
In leather-belted camel skin
Heaven's herald straightens desert pathways
Calling for the coming king;
Pouring waters of repentance
For an expectant generation
With warning words for those who see themselves
As God's elected nation.
'He who will come after,
More powerful than I,
With baptism of holy fire,
Whose shoes I am not worthy to untie.'

See also Mark 1:1-8, Luke 3:1-18 and John 1:19-28

10

Jordan's water
Matthew 3:13-17

Then Jesus came from Galilee to the Jordan to be baptised by John.

Matthew 3:13

Two men conjoined by destiny,
Revealer and revealed,
Preparer and the way, whose time has come
To be no more concealed.
Down endless generations
From Adam to the Christ,
The path of destiny unfolds
Regardless of the price.
Jordan's waters part once more;
This time, not as a prelude to war,
But God's loving exultation,
Whilst enemies conspire
Like pious snakes,
And claim their chosen station.
And so begins a public life
For God made flesh
Amongst his holy nation,
Though spurned at source
By those whose promises
He came to fill
Brim full
With water of salvation.

See also Mark 1:9-11, Luke 3:21-38 and John 1:29-34

11

Desert's end

Matthew 4:1-17

Jesus answered him, 'It is also written: "Do not put the Lord your God to the test."'

Matthew 4:7

In the desert of the soul
The Son of God must choose
To shelter in the vanities of man
Or follow faithfully his Father's plan.
This time no earthly garden of delights,
Just rock and dust and deepest hunger,
Forty days and forty nights.
Temptations prowl like angry beasts
To snare and lead astray
But scripture's words the surest guide
To him who is the way.
And he who has no home to call his own
Returns from desert trial
To be the very bread of life –
The end to man's exile.

See also Mark 1:12-15, Luke 4:1-15 and John 4:43-45

Ministry

12

Followers

John 1:35-51

The first thing Andrew did was to find his brother Simon and tell him, 'We have found the Messiah' (that is, the Christ). And he brought him to Jesus.

John 1:41-42a

Walking at the water's edge
Four followers are called to fish for men;
Each brother to another
And witness to the coming kingdom.
Setting out for deeper waters
Where faith is found,
The call to follow
Lies hidden in a breaking net.
Galilean fields prove fertile ground
For friends for whom God's word of old proves true,
As 'Moses' law made flesh' calls forth a man in whom
Nothing of falsehood can be found;
And words of prophecy foretell
Of heaven open through the Son of Man
For all who come hereafter
In faith-filled following.

See also Mark 1:16-20, Matthew 4:18-22 and Luke 5:1-11

13

Capernaum's time
Mark 1:21-39

'Be quiet!' said Jesus sternly. 'Come out of him!' The impure spirit shook the
man violently and came out of him with a shriek.

Mark 1:25

Capernaum, by Galilee's shore,
Home of men
Who will learn to fish for souls
In the power of God's Spirit,
In years
As yet untold;
For now, to sit at authority's feet
In scripture's school,
Where evil and madness
Are subject to his kingdom rule.
And later, that same power
Cupped in healing hands
Lifts a mother from her sickbed
To serve her sons.
Then in prayer before the dawn
To seek his Father's face
And thence set forth to Galilee
With Spirit's power and boundless grace.

See also Matthew 4:23-25; 8:14-17 and Luke 4:31-44

14

Cana

John 2:1-11

On the third day a wedding took place at Cana in Galilee.

John 2:1a

The first sign of the times
Glimpsed in the swirl of human celebration
With song and dance and food and wine,
New union, new creation.
The best new wine flows on,
Abundant beyond measure,
True sign of life to come,
This world – God's greatest treasure.
So too the final wedding
Whose time has not yet come,
With Christ revealed in glory
Seated high upon his throne;
Bridegroom and bride together,
Redemption plan complete,
The banquet table laid for all,
Where grace and justice meet.

15

Nicodemus
John 3:1-21

'How can someone be born when they are old?' Nicodemus asked. 'Surely they cannot enter a second time into their mother's womb to be born!'

John 3:4

Conversation with this man of God
In the shadowed depth of night
Sheds light into his darkened mind
That he might believe and truly find
The depth of love that gives eternal life.
Second birth the kingdom's key,
Abundant life the prize,
Blowing in the holy wind
For all with eyes
To see.
Israel's teacher hearing truth
Of earthly things and more
From him who stands where God commands
And none have gone before.

16

Bridegroom's voice
John 3:22-36

'He must become greater; I must become less.'

John 3:30

The time is fast approaching when
The herald of the kingdom steps aside,
To yield his place to him who must come after,
Greater by far than all mankind
   in history's pomp and pride.
And he who hears his Maker knows his work is done,
Yet still points forward into time –
   to things so soon to come.
The kingdom choice awaits for all,
For all lie in his hands,
God's Spirit without limit
Poured out at his command.
To bring abundant life and light
Lies in our very choice:
To turn and walk away
Or heed the Bridegroom's voice.

17

Rebukes and questions
Luke 3:19-20

But when John rebuked Herod the tetrarch because of his marriage to Herodias, his brother's wife, and all the other evil things he had done, Herod added this to them all: he locked John up in prison.

Luke 3:19-20

God's prophets down the ages
Speaking divine truth to earthly power
Stand weak but strong
In the heat of battle.
Nathan in his time
Rebuked the king
With wisdom's words;
So, too, John must face down sin.
But now no tearful grief
In tetrarch's tyrant hands,
As arrows once pierced a kingly heart,
But harsh retaliation and a prison cell;
And in the dark the doubts and questions start.
Is he Messiah? Who can tell?

18

I am he
John 4:1-42

'God is spirit, and his worshippers must worship in the Spirit and in truth.'

John 4:24

Seated, tired and thirsty,
God-made-man waits for water from a sinner's hand,
Whilst from his outstretched arms
Pours living water from the well of grace,
To nourish and sustain eternity.
The spirit of Sychar's mountain
Is as nothing to the heart of man
Bowed down in adoration
To the Father of us all.
True worship of the soul
Births new life in hearts grown cold.
Come and meet the man who knows
All that we have done,
Seated hungry and alone
And waiting at the well's edge
To bring his harvest home.

19

Second sign
John 4:46-54

This was the second sign Jesus performed after coming from Judea to Galilee.

John 4:54

Full twenty miles this walk of faith
Which ends on dusty knees,
Undignified before the man
He knows will hear his pleas.
A loving father most of all,
Who sees his son will die,
So stoops to beg for healing hands,
A sign from God on high.
'Your son will live,' the Lord declares;
The man in faith departs,
And on the roadway homeward
Hears news to lift his heart.
'Your son's alive,' his servants say,
'Upon the seventh hour' –
The very time that Jesus spoke
His words of healing power.

20

If

Mark 1:40-45

A man with leprosy came to him and begged him on his knees, 'If you are willing, you can make me clean.'

Mark 1:40

Our fainting faith prays 'if'
With doubt and hope in equal measure,
And with his gentle touch upon our frame
We know we are his dearest treasure.
Filled with love his voice responds, 'Be clean,'
And in an instant no sign of leprous sin is seen.
Christ the great physician, the healer of the world,
Who brings an end to sin and death –
His kingdom flag unfurled;
Yet not to bring him power and fame
Or all the praise of man,
But launch the overthrow of death,
This is the Master's plan.
And so to lonely places
Goes the king without a home,
To seek and meet his Father
And the fearful final pathway
To his cruel wooden throne.

See also Matthew 8:1-4 and Luke 5:12-16

21

Paralytic
Mark 2:1-12

'Which is easier: to say to this paralysed man, "Your sins are forgiven," or to say, "Get up, take your mat and walk"?'

Mark 2:9

Lying on the dirty linen stretcher of my life,
Carried by the lover of my soul;
Pressing through the throng of those
Who see but yet with blinded eyes,
Who hear yet do not know the song.
And so I come,
Through grace alone, not fit to kiss the feet
Of servant king upon his throne,
To hear his words of healing power
That wipe away all hurt and pain,
To know that all once lost is now my gain,
And rising from my sickness bed
To homeward walk – no longer dead,
With scripture's words and kingdom life
My holy,
Daily bread.

See also Matthew 9:1-8 and Luke 5:17-26

22

Dining with the Master
Matthew 9:9-17

'But go and learn what this means: "I desire mercy, not sacrifice." For I have not come to call the righteous, but sinners.'

Matthew 9:13

Rogues and vagabonds alike
Gather round Matthew's table
For a dinner with a difference,
With the Master of the universe
Born in flesh and blood and bone.
Whilst the high and mighty sniff and sneer
And trumpet their self-imposed piety,
And those imprisoned by the burdens of repentance
Struggle to see salvation in the healer's hands,
Sinners join the wedding feast,
Born into the light of new living.
All now is changed in God's new order
Down through time,
Across all generations
New life, new wine.
The bridegroom calls,
'Take up your mat
And walk!'

See also Mark 2:13-22 and Luke 5:27-39

23

Rule-breaker
John 5:1-47

In his defence Jesus said to them, 'My Father is always at his work to this very day, and I too am working.'

John 5:17

Trapped in deeper need than waters of Bethesda's pool
For nigh on forty years,
This invalid has lain in colonnaded poverty
Awaiting help that never came.
Then words of plain command
To rise and walk
Set free this lifelong prisoner
From chains of helplessness,
To stride the sabbath in new-found life.
Fulfilment of prophecies from ages past
Bear witness to the coming kingdom,
As Son and Saviour
In full obedience to the Father's will
Speaks truth to minds confined
By rigid rules of man-made law
Disguised as piety.

24

Destiny's walk

Matthew 12:1-21

Then he said to the man, 'Stretch out your hand.' So he stretched it out and it was completely restored, just as sound as the other. But the Pharisees went out and plotted how they might kill Jesus.

Matthew 12:13-14

Ritual, rule and doctrine suffocate the spirit
And stifle souls in search of freedom.
The teachers of the law
Preach and preen their legalism,
Hearts hardened like temple stones
Shaped for symbolism and sabbath sacrifice,
But merciless,
Devoid of love.
Shrivelled hand made whole
Whispers healing in the face of dogma.
The chosen servant,
Lord of the sabbath,
Unknown amongst his own,
Delights his Father
And walks through fields ripe for harvest
Towards his destiny.

See also Mark 2:23-3:12 and Luke 6:1-11

25

Eternity's echoes
Mark 3:13-19

Jesus went up on a mountainside and called to him those he wanted, and they came to him. He appointed twelve that they might be with him and that he might send them out to preach...

Mark 3:13-14

Twelve sons of Israel,
Shepherds on a Canaan hillside,
Patriarchs of an ancient people,
God's chosen nation;
And in their number
Those who would betray their brother
Who is soon their Saviour
And still retain his deep
Undying love.
Twelve sons of Israel
Gathered on a Galilean hillside
Hear their calling as messengers of
God's coming kingdom;
And in their midst
The man who would betray his master
Who is soon our Saviour
And still retain his deep
Undying love.

See also Luke 6:12-16

26

Attitudes
Matthew 5:1-20

'Blessed are you when people insult you, persecute you and falsely say all kinds of evil against you because of me. Rejoice and be glad, because great is your reward in heaven, for in the same way they persecuted the prophets who were before you.'

Matthew 5:11-12

Hillside seating makes
An amphitheatre for teaching
Attitudes of being
And kingdom living:
Salt of earth
And light of life,
Clothed in flesh
And word of mouth;
Fulfilling laws grown old
And hearts gone cold
With endless repetition;
A world turned upside-down
Where first is last
And greatest least,
Where rule and ritual are dead
And all are welcome at the kingdom feast.

See also Luke 6:17-26; 11:33-36

27

The price of heaven
Matthew 5:21-48

'If your right eye causes you to stumble, gouge it out and throw it away. It is better for you to lose one part of your body than for your whole body to be thrown into hell.'

Matthew 5:29

Severed arms and gouged-out eyes,
The price of gaining heaven's prize.
Avoid all anger,
Keep your word,
Give all away
And love without reward.
The law is but a shadow
Of perfection yet to come,
Not a measure of performance
Of just how well you've done.
Christ on the hillside
Heaven describes,
Kingdom values
Life, not lies.
No deception,
No pretence,
God of love
Not human sense.
And perfect love
In one man came
To rescue all
From sin and shame.
In him alone,
The path he trod,
For nothing is impossible
For God.

See also Luke 6:27-36

28

The Son's prayer
Matthew 6:1-18

'This, then, is how you should pray...'

Matthew 6:9a

God of the heart,
Of motive and the hidden self,
Not outward piety
Or showy duty
That trumpets spiritual superiority
In the face of need.
Humility and selfless love
Worked in secret,
Not disfigured by a sanctimonious
Public faith,
But unknown to all but God
And bathed in holy oil and prayer.
Father of us all,
Your name is holiness itself;
Your kingdom comes
In the faith of your followers,
Whom you forgive
And save from evil.
So do not fear
To seek God out.
The bread of life is free;
Even deep in darkest night,
Boldness
Is the key.

See also Luke 11:1-8

29

True treasures

Matthew 6:19-34

'Therefore do not worry about tomorrow, for tomorrow will worry about itself. Each day has enough trouble of its own.'

Matthew 6:34

Worry at the heart of man
Corrodes the soul
Like rusting treasure trove
Buried beneath the deep dark earth
Of human self-reliance;
The cares of life
The manacles of man's own making.
But let in the light of faith
Through the soul's eye
And fears fade
With the dawn's new song,
Like morning mist
On meadow flowers,
Bathed in the sun's bright rising.

See also Luke 12:22-34

30

Hillside stories

Matthew 7:1-14

'Enter through the narrow gate. For wide is the gate and broad is the road that leads to destruction, and many enter through it. But small is the gate and narrow the road that leads to life, and only a few find it.'

Matthew 7:13-14

Stories told on a sunlit hill
Lay firm foundations
For storms in life
And tests of will.
Tales of dust and wood
And pearls and pigs,
Of bread and stones,
Of thorns and figs;
And as these tales of life unfold,
The smallest gate
Stands at the bend
On the narrow road.
So walk the path
That few may find.
To all who ask
And seek
And knock
His kingdom comes,
His love is kind.

See also Luke 6:37-42; 11:9-13

31

Foundations
Matthew 7:15-29

'Therefore everyone who hears these words of mine and puts them into practice is like a wise man who built his house on the rock.'

Matthew 7:24

Ears tingle at prophetic words
Spoken by wolves in sheep's clothing,
Bearing false and toxic fruit
Fit only for the final furnace.
Across the arc of history
The ancient empires of mankind
In grand design
Now crouch in ruins,
Silent and irrelevant;
Mere relics of their long-abandoned past.
Whilst the living word of God
Flows ever onward;
Wisdom's river whose stone foundation
Lies undisturbed by the passing floods of time
Which wash away the sands of human foolishness
In wave-tossed waters.

See also Luke 6:43-49

32

Greater faith
Luke 7:1-10

So Jesus went with them. He was not far from the house when the centurion sent friends to say to him: 'Lord, don't trouble yourself, for I do not deserve to have you come under my roof.'

Luke 7:6

A man in a hundred with greater faith than all in Israel
Begs for healing at the Messiah's word,
For his own suffering servant
Whose need for grace and healing his heart has heard.
'Lord, I am not worthy,'
   are the words for which he's known,
And he who hears our every prayer
   sends healing speeding home;
Words we all can echo for we know our helpless state,
But God ignores our sinfulness, his grace is at the gate;
Available to all – of every creed and clan,
Both Jew and gentile, slave and free.
Grace without a limit
Poured out for you and me;
No longer sick and dying but freed by grace alone
To live his life abundant in this new kingdom home.

See also Matthew 8:5-13

33

Nain

Luke 7:11-17

Then he went up and touched the bier they were carrying him on, and the bearers stood still. He said, 'Young man, I say to you, get up!' The dead man sat up and began to talk, and Jesus gave him back to his mother.

Luke 7:14-15

Crowds press in and hem on every side
As Christ encounters death held high;
Her only son, her precious one,
Her grief too deep to try
Mere words of consolation.
Yet even the unreachable are his;
With simple touch and sweet command
From him who is the Son of God
Grief and death itself are banned,
God's power for his nation.
'A prophet is amongst us,'
The news from Nain
Soon spreads abroad,
This young man raised to life
By just a simple word;
True sign of our salvation.

34

Soul lessons
Matthew 11:1-30

...Jesus said, 'I praise you, Father, Lord of heaven and earth, because you have hidden these things from the wise and learned, and revealed them to little children. Yes, Father, for this is what you were pleased to do.'

Matthew 11:25-26

As wisdom is proved right by deeds,
The prophet doubts from prison cell;
His chosen children ask his name
   as dead are raised and sick made well.
Like curtains drawn across blind eyes
The doubly deaf choose not to hear
As miracles pour forth from him
   whose acts of love show heaven draws near.
Such things are hidden from the wise
For God's good pleasure, nothing more,
And children find such treasure here
   revealed in Christ through love not law.
So come to him and find true rest;
His yoke is easy, burden light,
For humbleness of heart is all we need
   to learn for soul's delight.

See also Luke 7:18-35

35

Disciples
Luke 8:1-3

These women were helping to support them out of their own means.

Luke 8:3b

Women of Christ,
True followers,
Walk the path of Palestine and life
To story's bitter end.
With the twelve they travel prepared to give
The all they have
In heaven's sweet pursuit;
Give all their means to reach the end.
This is their calling and our blessed memory
Inscribed on scripture's page for all to see.
And in the coming kingdom
To know their loud 'Amen!'

36

Divided houses

Matthew 12:22-45

Jesus knew their thoughts and said to them, 'Every kingdom divided against itself will be ruined, and every city or household divided against itself will not stand.'

Matthew 12:25

From overflowing hearts
Pours good and bad
Through mouths that speak
The inner man.
And Jesus reads our every thought,
Our heart,
Our soul,
The sin we plan.
The wrath of God will conquer all,
Divided houses cannot stand.
As jackals of the desert,
Sweet oiled tongues of religious men
Beseech another sign from heaven's Son;
But he who knows their darkest thoughts
And knows the where, the why and when
Will answer give them none.
Yet grace will heal as we repent
And turn to him as God commands.
The Son of Man, like Jonah once,
In deepest dark will lay in death;
Then all, like Ninevah, will rise
At God's true word, his life, his breath.

See also Mark 3:20-30 and Luke 11:14-32

37

Family
Luke 8:19-21

'My mother and brothers are those who hear God's word and put it into practice.'

Luke 8:21

Born of woman.
Fully man.
The Son of God knows all the love of home
And yet is also deep alone.
For in his heart
He hears
His Father's call to save this world through love;
The word of God from heaven above.
And thus his words:
'Who then
Is mother to me or my kith and kin?
But those who hear and enter in…'
Will you?

See also Matthew 12:46-50 and Mark 3:31-35

38

Seeds
Mark 4:1-25

He told them, 'The secret of the kingdom of God has been given to you. But to those on the outside everything is said in parables...'

Mark 4:11

Seated at the lakeside,
Speaking tales of truth and grace
That fall like seeds into the heart of man
And yield their fruit in time and space.
For some, stories are soon forgot,
For others but a short while's careless thought.
For some a waste of space in life's harsh race,
Whilst those who hear and know its truth
Become fresh sowers in his place.
And as the Christ speaks out the word,
To grow and thrive a hundredfold,
The grace of God is shed abroad
Except in those whose hearts are cold.
In them, the prophecy fulfilled
Of those who won't turn to be healed,
Blind eyes,
Deaf ears,
Hard hearts,
Life's tears.
Whilst all around the kingdom grows
Beknown to God from whom grace flows.

See also Matthew 13:1-23 and Luke 8:4-18

39

Hidden love
Matthew 13:24-52

He said to them, 'Therefore every teacher of the law who has become a disciple in the kingdom of heaven is like the owner of a house who brings out of his storeroom new treasures as well as old.'

Matthew 13:52

A prophet in his own town scorned
By those who knew him best of all
Tells stories to the least of men
Who crowd around to hear his call.
These tales of fish and pearls and weeds
And trees that grow from mustard seeds
Point to God's kingdom all around
Which sought with purpose can be found,
Like yeast in dough that leavens bread,
Or treasure hidden in a field,
Or seeds and weeds together grown,
So, too, is gracious love concealed.
And all these kingdom stories tell
Of God's great love for every man,
Of kingdom's justice, truth and love
And rescue through salvation's plan.

See also Mark 4:26-34 and Luke 13:18-21

40

Stormy waters
Mark 4:35-41

They were terrified and asked each other, 'Who is this? Even the wind and the waves obey him!'

Mark 4:41

'Where is your faith?' I hear him ask of me.
'Why so easily afraid? Why so often all at sea?
Why the waves of fear and doubt,
The winds of deep uncertainty?'
Asleep and just a breath away
My Lord and Saviour lies,
And wakes to calm the storms of life,
Responding to my cries.
Like David deep in ages past,
Who knew both hurt and pain,
Surrendered all in praise and prayer
Offered in your name,
May so do I, and in the peace
That your awakening brings
Know that the wind and waves of life
Obey the king of kings.

See also Matthew 8:23-27 and Luke 8:22-25

41

Legion
Mark 5:1-20

As Jesus was getting into the boat, the man who had been demon-possessed begged to go with him. Jesus did not let him, but said, 'Go home to your own people and tell them how much the Lord has done for you, and how he has had mercy on you.'

Mark 5:18-19

Man of the Gerasenes, naked and alone,
Living yet dead, unchained but yet in darkness bound,
Deprived of mind
And captive of a thousand raging voices;
Then rising from his prison tomb
To stand before God's Most High Son
To face his demons and find true freedom.
This too our destiny in Christ,
Our rock and solid ground,
To know salvation in his name
And live to tell
How much the Lord has done.

See also Matthew 8:28-34 and Luke 8:26-39

42

Compassion
Matthew 9:18-38

She said to herself, 'If I only touch his cloak, I will be healed.'

Matthew 9:21

Healing in hands and feet,
His word, his clothing,
Powered by faith in those
Who seek his knowing.
Noisome crowds
Caught up in rights and rituals of dying
Shut out from the intimacy of resurrection,
Which beggars belief,
And catches demons unaware.
Sheep without a shepherd,
Vineyards without workers;
Compassion in the very dust and air.

See also Mark 55:21-43 and Luke 8:40-56

43

Rejection
Luke 4:16-30

'Truly I tell you,' he continued, 'no prophet is accepted in his home town.'

Luke 4:24

Scroll of the prophet unfurled by truth
Made flesh and blood and bone
In carpenter's guise,
Seated in their midst with words of grace
   that shocked the wise,
Who looked for signs and wonders
But not at any price,
As pride and disbelief
Shout down the gift of life.
Isaiah in his time
Had known rejection's call,
So, too, the man of whom he spoke
Will pay the price for all.
And so the man of sorrows
Slips silently away
To birth God's kingdom here on earth
Until that final fulfilled day.

See also Matthew 13:53-58, Mark 6:1-6
and John 4:43-45

44

The twelve
Matthew 10:1-42

'I am sending you out like sheep among wolves. Therefore be as shrewd as snakes and as innocent as doves.'

Matthew 10:16

Twelve followers
Seek the lost of Israel,
Shaking dust from tired feet;
Messengers of the coming kingdom
With gifts of healing,
Words of wisdom
And the Spirit of freedom,
Clothed in innocence and cunning.
Persecution surely follows
In the slipstream of salvation.
Hairs are counted,
Sparrows sold
And families fracture,
As cups of cold water are shared
With those in need.

See also Mark 6:7-13 and Luke 9:1-6

45

The Son
Matthew 14:1-36

*Immediately Jesus reached out his hand and caught him. 'You of little faith,'
he said, 'why did you doubt?'*

As tyrant king
The prophet priest beheads,
God-man of sea and mountain
Water treads
To catch a drowning soul
Whose faith has faltered.
Feeding full five thousand
From compassion's hands,
As doubters bring in baskets
Filled with fish and bread he broke,
Whilst sick on stretchers wait their moment
Clutching for his cloak.
And both before and in between,
Solitary;
In private prayer
With Father God whose love he lives,
Whose path he treads,
Towards his destiny as yet unseen.

See also Mark 6:14-56, Luke 9:7-17 and John 6:1-21

46

Food for life

John 6:22-71

'Whoever eats my flesh and drinks my blood has eternal life, and I will raise them up at the last day.'

John 6:54

Staff of life made flesh and blood,
True bread of heaven from God above.
This gift of grace too hard to hear;
Disciples leave who once drew near.
For what is free cannot be earned;
What Jesus gives, religion spurns
And asks for proof, in place of faith;
Not God of all but chosen race.
The twelve remain; where could they go?
His words made flesh they trust and know.
But one of them does not believe
And so his choice: betray – deceive.
Yet even here the Most High God
Ordained the path the Son has trod.

47

Dirty hands

Matthew 15:1-20

'"These people honour me with their lips, but their hearts are far from me. They worship me in vain; their teachings are merely human rules."'

Matthew 15:8-9

Cleanliness and godliness
Crafted into religion's icon
Distract mankind from what is really true.
Satan delights in endless washing of the outer self
Whilst inner darkness
Coils serpentine around the heart.
So, too, with all of man's made rules
That point to God,
Whilst not themselves the truth,
When followed mindlessly
Lead to legalism's rule
And pitfalls of our blind conceit.
Far better, then, to love your fellow man
And find true value
In purity of heart
And dirt-stained hands.

See also Mark 7:1-23

48

Soul food

Mark 7:24-8:10

He told the crowd to sit down on the ground. When he had taken the seven loaves and given thanks, he broke them and gave them to his disciples to distribute to the people, and they did so.

Mark 8:6

Four thousand fed on fish and bread
As Jesus' healing hands
Bring grace and wholeness
To all placed at his feet.
Compassion knows no borders
In the coming kingdom;
Whether dogs, blind men or chosen children,
All receive their portion
At the Master's table,
With basketfuls of broken pieces gathered in.
Such is the bounty
Of his redeeming love.

See also Matthew 15:21-39

49

Witnesses
Matthew 16:1-28

Jesus replied, 'Blessed are you, Simon son of Jonah, for this was not revealed to you by flesh and blood, but by my Father in heaven.'

Matthew 16:17

As both the sign of Jonah and his son
Bear witness to a doubting world
That Christ the Son of God has come,
His followers are all at sea
With talk of yeast and bread
And miss the point of what's been said:
That mercy, love and heartfelt faith
Lived in the Spirit
Matter more
Than all the ritual and rules imposed by men
Upon a people weary in the waiting.
Keys are given,
Promises are made,
And on this firm foundation,
On this rock,
Is laid
The guiltless Son of Man,
To lose his life to win us all
And so fulfil
God's perfect plan.

See also Mark 8:11-9:1 and Luke 9:18-27

50

Chosen Son

Luke 9:28-36

A voice came from the cloud, saying, 'This is my Son, whom I have chosen; listen to him.'

High on the mountain
Three followers behold the sight:
The Son of Man made glorious king
In royal robe of pure and whitest light.
Elijah, Moses either side
Caught in heaven's shining
As men lie face down to the ground
At this true Son's bright rising.
The voice of God is clearly heard,
Delighted in his Son;
This the moment, this the hour
And this my chosen one,
That every man from his own sin
Can finally be freed,
But first the call to hold to faith
As small as mustard seed.

See also Matthew 17:1-13 and Mark 9:2-13

51

Faith and doubt
Mark 9:14-32

'"If you can"?' said Jesus. 'Everything is possible for one who believes.'

Mark 9:23

Belief and unbelief,
Opposing twins conjoined since Eden
Wrestle for supremacy
At the heart of man.
Satan's ambassador makes men mute
As mustard seed faith, un-prayed-for,
Writhes parched and powerless
In the desert dust.
Yet even here,
Despite the faltering of a father's faith,
The Son of Man
Confounds and triumphs over death,
Whilst words
Of all too soon departing
Pass by
Unheard.

See also Matthew 17:14-23 and Luke 9:37-45; 17:5-6

52

Two drachma
Matthew 17:24-27

'Take the first fish you catch; open its mouth and you will find a four-drachma coin. Take it and give it to them for my tax and yours.'

Matthew 17:27b

Taxman's threats
Brings forth rash answers
And a king's question.
Whilst
A fish's mouth
Brings forth a silver shekel
And a royal ransom.

53

The greatest
Mark 9:33-50

'Whoever welcomes one of these little children in my name welcomes me; and whoever welcomes me does not welcome me but the one who sent me.'

Mark 9:37

In the midst of the crowd
The young child stands
Gazing up at those around
Whose human pride grasps all in vain
For status that cannot be found.
Whilst enemies are welcomed
With cups of water,
Those made great by grace
Through childlike faith,
Swing wide the doors of heaven
For half-blind shepherds
Hobbling homewards.

See also Matthew 18:1-14 and Luke 9:46-50; 17:1-2

54

Forgiveness
Matthew 18:15-35

*Then Peter came to Jesus and asked, 'Lord, how many times shall I forgive
my brother or sister who sins against me? Up to seven times?' Jesus answered,
'I tell you, not seven times, but seventy-seven times.'*

Matthew 18:21-22

The wreck of souls
Upon the rock of retribution;
For wrongs endured
Just punishment and restitution.
The Covenant of Law
Seeks rightly to address
The needs of man
In need of grace;
But grace himself walks now upon the earth
Forgiving all
Who seek his kingdom's truth.
No limit set
On love divine
For all are his,
All his are mine.

See also Luke 17:3-4

55

Divine destiny
Luke 9:51-62

Jesus replied, 'Foxes have dens and birds have nests, but the Son of Man has nowhere to lay his head.'

Luke 9:58

The long road homeward,
Where footsteps in the dust
Bring threats of fire from thunder's sons
Who choose not grace but strife.
But following this narrow path
Demands the greater price.
Both cross and crown are his to own
Who chose love's sacrifice.
No home or resting place,
No anguished backward gaze,
But steadfast walk to heaven's gate
Through these his final days.

See also Matthew 8:18-22

56

Divisions
John 7:1-52

'...but I know him because I am from him and he sent me.' At this they tried to seize him, but no one laid a hand on him, because his hour had not yet come.

John 7:29-30

This Son of Galilee,
Whose time has not yet come
In temple courts
Speaks out his Father's words
To all who gather to recall
Their nation's tented wandering.
Twin pillars,
Fire and cloud,
Lead homeward a complaining people
To their Promised Land.
And quarrelling still,
Messiah's words divide;
Some choose to follow, others cry
For divine retribution.
Like Meribah,
This cornerstone of living water
Poured out
For those who seek and find,
Whilst Sanhedrin squabble
And wisdom's words malign.

57

Dust

John 7:53-8:11

Jesus straightened up and asked her, 'Woman, where are they? Has no one condemned you?' 'No one, sir,' she said. 'Then neither do I condemn you,' Jesus declared. 'Go now and leave your life of sin.'

John 8:10-11

Calloused finger in the dust,
The Son of Man stooped down
To hear the accusation
Of the so-called 'just'
Who twist the law to vindicate
Their righteous indignation.
But dust is where we come from,
To dust all will return,
And all who seek the highest place
Must bow before his throne;
And condemnation is there none
But mercy without end,
For grace has paid the price for all
In innocence condemned.
Calloused hands will carry
The guilt of all mankind
So we can leave our life of sin
And freedom truly find.

58

Old and new
John 8:12-59

'...if the Son sets you free, you will be free indeed.'

John 8:36

The pharisees and scribes
Debate the finer points of law
And elevate
Their knowledge of the Covenant above the needs
Of poorest of the poor.
These sons of Abraham proclaim
Their piety and pride
In chosen status before God
Whilst slaves to sin inside.
The light of life, the great I AM,
The Son who sets us free,
The truth of God
Made flesh and blood, new Covenant of grace and love
He only holds the key.
And so to rocks and stones they turn
With hatred and with scorn
To silence him who had no sin
Whose time had not yet come.

59

God's messengers
Luke 10:1-24

The seventy-two returned with joy and said, 'Lord, even the demons submit to us in your name.' He replied, 'I saw Satan fall like lightning from heaven.'

Luke 10:17-18

Barefoot heralds of the coming kingdom,
Both followers and followed,
Walk the dust of Palestine
Clothed in the Spirit of God.
Peace and healing pouring forth
In equal measure,
With prophecy and warning
For all who fail to see this kingdom's treasure.
Salvation written in the Book of Life
Brings joy unbound
According to the Father's pleasure.
Blind eyes don't see,
Deaf ears don't hear,
As Satan falls and heaven draws near.

60

Samaritans
Luke 10:25-37

'Which of these three do you think was a neighbour to the man who fell into the hands of robbers?'

Luke 10:36

Walking on life's path,
Mankind is set upon
And robbed of all he owns,
Then left beside the road
Incapable,
Awaiting death – alone.
Here God himself searches for us
With healing and his grace,
To salve our wounds, to bring us home;
He pays the price and takes our place.
So all are neighbours – all in need,
A world with outstretched hands;
And so to 'go and likewise do',
This is his great command

61

Bethany's cares

Luke 10:38-42

'Martha, Martha,' the Lord answered, 'you are worried and upset about many things, but few things are needed – or indeed only one. Mary has chosen what is better, and it will not be taken away from her.'

Luke 10:41-42

Cares and work are many
Pressing in upon each day,
Stealing life like ebbing tide
Or river's flood,
Never to return.
But love's full blessing,
Captured in his double calling
Of her name
Breaks deep waters of rebirth
On a life's hard serving
And newfound worship
At her Saviour's feet.

62

Blind guides

Luke 11:37-54

'Woe to you experts in the law, because you have taken away the key to knowledge. You yourselves have not entered, and you have hindered those who were entering.'

Luke 11:52

Scrupulous and principled
Upon each minor point of law,
Fastidious and faithful,
Yet heartless to the poor.
The paragons of piety
Who seek the highest seat,
Yet will not lift one finger
For the beggar in the street.
Blind guides who steal the key of life
And will not enter in,
Yet hinder those who seek to find
The end to all their sin.
And so the woes and foolishness
Of man's religious plight
Still fail to grasp the heart of God
That's hidden in plain sight.

63

Fear not

Luke 12:1-12

'Indeed, the very hairs of your head are all numbered. Don't be afraid; you are worth more than many sparrows.'

Luke 12:7

The triumph of the unimpressive
before the courts of rulers and self-righteous
Is prophesied on a crowded hill,
Where fear and curiosity
Trample the weakest underfoot.
Caged sparrows know his favour
As hairy heads are counted
And whispered words
Concealed in darkened rooms
Are shouted from the rooftops.
The love of God
Is the measure of mankind,
And fear has no hiding place
For those who trust in him
And know his guiding Spirit.

64

Inheritance
Luke 12:13-21

Then he said to them, 'Watch out! Be on your guard against all kinds of greed; life does not consist in an abundance of possessions.'

Luke 12:15

Life is fleeting, time is short;
The urge to build and save,
To store, accumulate and hoard,
Is ended by the grave.
To honour God and love the world,
Here lies the greater prize,
Not selfish gain in gold or grain
These mere foolish lies.
They lure the heart and snare the soul,
Deception every one.
True fear of God and love for man
Will see his kingdom come.
So choose a true inheritance
Whose goodness will endure
And see God's kingdom riches here
Both now and evermore.

65

Future's end
Luke 12:35-13:9

'You also must be ready, because the Son of Man will come at an hour when you do not expect him.'

Luke 12:40

The tide of time will turn,
Inexorable;
Yet none can know the hour
Of the Master's soon return.
So tales of servants, banquets
And a fruitless fig tree
Soft foretell
The call to watchful waiting
And the Father's will.
But even such soul-speaking
Burns as fire
As storm clouds gather
And families divide
At the rim of repentance.

See also Luke 17:7-10

66

Unbound

Luke 13:10-17

Then he put his hands on her, and immediately she straightened up...

Luke 13:13a

A life bowed down,
Heaven out of reach or gaze,
Staring at the earth's dry ground,
Barred from sharing prayer or praise.
This the circumstance of all,
The prison cage of man,
Until the voice of Christ calls forth
With healing in his hands.
Now standing upright face to face
Through Christ our Saviour, by his grace,
Whose endless love is greater than
The sabbath rules imposed by man.

86

67

Siloam's water

John 9:1-41

'You were steeped in sin at birth; how dare you lecture us!' And they threw him out.

John 9:34b

The love of God
For blameless generations
Of a world born blind,
Revealed in sabbath mud and spit
And Siloam's silent waters.
But none so blind
As those who will not see
Their claim to earn their place
Is but their human vanity;
Who seek to steep again in sin
Those whom the grace of Christ
Set free.

68

Gatekeeper
John 10:1-21

'The reason my Father loves me is that I lay down my life – only to take it up again. No one takes it from me, but I lay it down of my own accord. I have authority to lay it down and authority to take it up again.'

John 10:17-18a

Enter through the gate of God,
His sole begotten Son;
The way, the truth, the life are his,
And he the only one.
The shepherd and the watchman,
The keeper and the gate;
A mystery too deep for words
Yet mankind's glorious fate.
The shepherd and the sheep
Who know the Master's voice,
As Father knows his only Son
And love's redeeming choice.
Beloved of all creation
By the lover of the lost,
Who came to seek and rescue
Regardless of the cost;
To lay his life down for all sin,
To pay the perfect price
And take it up again for all,
Our servant king, our Christ.

69

Dedication
John 10:22-42

'I and the Father are one.'

John 10:30

The Feast of Dedication,
The Temple Mount renewed
And God again is present
Yet now in full and human view.
Surrounded in the colonnade he tells
That 'he and I are one',
This Saviour in a pauper's garb
Who claims he is the Father's Son;
And points to miracles and signs
As testament of truth,
But blindness born of blasphemy
Won't tolerate such proof.
So the Father's dedication
To his eternal plan
Rests by the Jordan waters
In Christ the Son of Man.

89

70

The narrow door

Luke 13:22-30

'People will come from east and west and north and south, and will take their places at the feast in the kingdom of God.'

Luke 13:29

Search and find the narrow door,
The path to kingdom blessings without end,
As servant Son awaits with open arms
To welcome all
Who walk his long road home.
Jerusalem portends both coming end
And new beginning;
The gathering of all who know the grace
Of sins forgiving,
And so stand tall in heaven's hall
To bless the one who comes
In Yahweh's name.

71

Exchange
Luke 14:1-24

'For all those who exalt themselves will be humbled, and those who humble themselves will be exalted.'

Luke 14:11

The pompous and self-righteous
Who mistake entitlement for grace,
Whose hearts are slave to public recognition
And seek what they perceive as their anointed place,
Are deaf to heaven's invitation
   to the wedding of the Lamb
And look instead to worldly wealth
And all the schemes of mammon and
Of man.
So heaven's place is given to the weakest and the poor,
The sick, the lame and blinded
Who lie beyond the temple's door;
And so the first and last
Exchange places at the feast,
The poorest for the richest,
The greatest for the least.

72

Life's journey
Luke 14:25-35

'And whoever does not carry their cross and follow me cannot be my disciple.'

The cost of faithful following
Encountered in the cross of life
Births brightest hope
Made light by grace.
Salt rubbed in chaffed relationships
Heals despite the hurts
And spurs all on to run the race
Of human destiny;
Whilst he who goes before
Travels as protecting guide
To welcome us with open arms
At journey's end.

73

Found
Luke 15:1-32

'But while he was still a long way off, his father saw him and was filled with compassion for him; he ran to his son, threw his arms round him and kissed him.'

Luke 15:20b

Pillars of self-righteousness
Murmur at the margin,
Whilst those know
Their utter need of grace
Clamour to be close.
Tales of lost and found
Speak kingdom's paradox
To those who sit on holy ground
To feel the touch and hear
The words of God-made-man;
Our Father
Running to the world's end
To welcome home his great creation
To their true inheritance.

74

True riches

Luke 16:1-31

'So if you have not been trustworthy in handling worldly wealth, who will trust you with true riches?'

Luke 16:11

The snare of money, stronger than the human will,
Deceives the heart with promises it can't fulfil;
The urge to gather, store and hoard
Conceals itself as right reward
And wealth hard won,
So what should be an instrument of grace
Becomes a tyrant master in God's place.
And Mammon feeds our human greed
Disguising want as rightful need,
An all-consuming one!
But heaven's riches lie in servant guise
To give away – love's greater prize;
Abundant life the rich reward
In serving Jesus Christ our Lord,
The Father's righteous one.
So look to be an instrument of grace,
His hands and feet with human face;
Seek first to serve our neighbours' needs
And put aside our selfish greed
In following his Son.

75

Life and death
John 11:1-57

Jesus said to her, 'I am the resurrection and the life. The one who believes in me will live, even though they die...'

John 11:25

Lazarus, beloved brother called by God,
Sleeps four days deep in tomb's enclosing walls,
As sisters weep and Saviour waits
The Father's whispered call.
Grief and grace entwine
With promises of resurrection power,
Washed in compassion's tears
At Bethany's door.
Faith is built upon the rock
Of death defeated in plain sight;
Grave clothes unwind
As dark gives way to life's new light.
Yet even here the pride of man is great
And whispered words
In corridors of power
Foretell of murder born of hate.

76

Ten

Luke 17:11-19

Jesus asked, 'Were not all ten cleansed? Where are the other nine?'

Luke 17:17

Outcast's scourge made visible in flesh,
Calls out for pity's sake
Beyond the border's edge,
As Christ walks south
To meet his destiny with death.
And as these ten,
So, too, are we to walk in faith
And know his healing
On the path of life,
Then
As the one who swift returns,
Give thanks to God
And rise to share this miracle
Of grace
In lifelong testament
Of him who saves.

77

Coming kingdom
Luke 17:20-37

'... nor will people say, "Here it is," or "There it is," because the kingdom of God is in your midst.'

Luke 17:21

Where vultures gather
Dead men rise
To meet their Saviour
In the skies;
With earth remade
As heaven's prize
No grief, no tears,
No greed, no lies.
His kingdom comes
In softest guise
To grace the hearts
Of all those wise
Enough to see
With faithful eyes
That love is God's
Great enterprise.

78

Persistence
Luke 18:1-8

'And will not God bring about justice for his chosen ones, who cry out to him day and night?'

Luke 18:7a

A life of faith lived out in prayerful walk
Before the Lord of all
Births character and hope
Inside our human soul.
Our cries for justice, peace and love
Ascend to heaven's throne
And move the very heart of God
To see sin overthrown.
But when the Son of Man returns
To bring the world's rebirth,
Will kingdom praise be heard at all
Or faith persist on earth?

79

Two prayers
Luke 18:9-14

'For all those who exalt themselves will be humbled, and those who humble themselves will be exalted.'

Self-righteousness and pride
Lurk like lions at ego's door
Intent on self-aggrandisement
And dark complacency;
Beneath the grubby robe
Of public piety and outspoken prayer,
A heart of granite
From which no mercy flows.
Whilst in the shadow of his wings
Is grace to bow with grateful heart,
To know that mercy is not earned,
And righteousness the gift
Of matchless love.
No sin of man prevails,
Save that which fails
To see its own deceit.

80

Love
Matthew 19:1-12

'...at the beginning the Creator "made them male and female"...'

Matthew 19:4

Love is the very heart of God,
And in his great creation
Breathes his image
Cast in flesh and blood;
For lifelong love as equals
Yet each their own.
And thus the mystery of life
Conceived of human passion,
Two as one;
Bearing the likeness
Of their Maker
Down countless generations.

See also Mark 10:1-12

81

Carpenter's hands

Mark 10:13-16

And he took the children in his arms, placed his hands on them and blessed them.

Mark 10:16

Outstretched arms
Meet a carpenter's scarred hands;
Blessing and forgiveness
That sin cannot withstand.
As fervent followers
Strive to keep the poor at bay,
The Saviour of mankind
Proclaims a different way:
The path of grace and welcome
To all who seek his face,
Of kingdom's new beginning
And heaven's earthly place.
For God so loves the world
He sent his only Son.
For all who trust in Jesus' name
His kingdom now has come.

See also Matthew 19:13-15 and Luke 18:15-17

82

Life-giving treasure
Matthew 19:16-30

Just then a man came up to Jesus and asked, 'Teacher, what good thing must I do to get eternal life?'

Matthew 19:16

The young man so keen to seek the path of life,
Or so it seems,
Observing well the duties of his role
But holding fast to money's dreams,
Stands heart unbowed before the Lord,
Commandments kept but love ignored.
The grip of earthly treasures,
Like manacles around his heart,
Bring loss and sadness in their wake
As all stand watching him depart.
For the blessings of the kingdom
Lie beyond the needle's eye,
Impossible for man to reach
But there for all
Through God's own Son,
Who lives for us
Yet came to die.
For first is last
And loss is gain,
His death our life
In heaven's domain.

See also Mark 10:17-31 and Luke 18:18-30

83

Equality

Matthew 20:1-16

'So the last will be first, and the first will be last.'

Matthew 20:16

Favoured sons by race and long tradition,
Puffed up by pious rules and strict religion,
No doubt believe theirs is the favoured place,
The seat of honour by right – not grace.
It's they who've worked their faith to death
And damned all others in word and breath.
They have earned the highest prize
To gaze at others through pride's pale eyes.
But Jesus knows the hidden soul;
He sees the hardened heart and cold
Hard logic of this stony rule,
Where grace is hidden and laws are cruel.
Yet God's great love ignores it all,
He lifts all up and all stand tall.
No matter how we come to him,
Or why or who or where or when,
The great reward is just the same:
Abundant life,
The great exchange.

84

Fearful mystery
Mark 10:32-34

They were on their way up to Jerusalem, with Jesus leading the way, and the disciples were astonished, while those who followed were afraid.

Mark 10:32a

Hidden messages
Too soon to know or understand;
The fast-approaching dark of human sin
Will overwhelm the servant king,
Yet this is God's eternal plan.
These followers of footsteps in Galilean dust
Are called to walk in history,
To live by faith and trust
That he who goes before them,
He only knows the way
And they will keep his company
Until that frightful day.
But promises of soon return
Are also spoken here
Concealed within the passion
Of God's love
And human fear.

See also Matthew 20:17-19 and Luke 18:31-34

85

Blindness
Matthew 20:20-34

Jesus said to them, 'You will indeed drink from my cup, but to sit at my right or left is not for me to grant. These places belong to those for whom they have been prepared by my Father.'

Matthew 20:23

Blind ambition leads to special pleading
On a mother's bended knee,
For kingdom thrones both left and right,
The price of which cannot be earned or seen;
But given by the Father to the servants of us all.
The greatest in his kingdom
Like beggars on the road,
Pleading in the dark for eyes to see,
Who know the healing of his hands
And the depth of his compassion.

See also Mark 10:35-52 and Luke 18:35-43

86

God's taxman
Luke 19:1-10

Jesus said to him, 'Today salvation has come to this house, because this man, too, is a son of Abraham.'

Luke 19:9

This son of Abraham
Caught in the crowd of unknowing
And simply curious,
Climbs high
To see the Son of Man
Walk by,
And in the seeing
Comes to know
The welcome of a prodigal's return,
Of sin's forgiveness
And sweet salvation.
A little man
Made great
In the branches of a tree
Which stands at heaven's gate.

87

Minas' tale
Luke 19:11-27

'He replied, "I tell you that to everyone who has, more will be given, but as for the one who has nothing, even what they have will be taken away."'

Luke 19:26

A life well lived
Captured in this kingdom's cautionary tale,
Of grace received and shared
And at its ending just reward,
Stands contrast
To our need to hide and hoard
In vain pursuit of earth-bound treasures
Which will be cast away
When comes the time to stand before the Lord;
For life is more than minas
And death no more
Than new life's open door.

88

God's heart
Matthew 26:1-16

*While Jesus was in Bethany in the home of Simon the Leper, a woman came
to him with an alabaster jar of very expensive perfume, which she poured on
his head as he was reclining at the table.*

Matthew 26:6-7

Quietly she comes with alabaster jar
Of deepest love and tears of joy.
Pouring oil of anointing,
Signs of death and brother's resurrection.
Silently he goes with emptied heart
Of thwarted plans and revolution's rage.
And in the shadows
Between them both,
The rulers plot and scheme
The ending of this Rabbi,
And God's fulfilment
As yet unseen.

*See also Mark 14:1-11, Luke 7:36-50; 22:1-6
and John 12:1-11*

Passion, Death and Resurrection

89

Fig tree faith
Mark 11:1-26

'Truly I tell you, if anyone says to this mountain, "Go, throw yourself into the sea," and does not doubt in their heart but believes that what they say will happen, it will be done for them.'

Mark 11:23

The fig tree faithful,
Leaves and branches raised in praise
To the Son of David on a donkey's colt –
Yet fruitless –
Will wither and die in the heat of persecution
So soon to come.
Meanwhile, tables are turned
And doves set free;
The sick find healing in his wings
And the blind can see.
As children sing, 'Hosannah!'
In the debris of dead religion,
He whose faith can move a mountain
Faces death for our salvation.

See also Matthew 21:1-22, Luke 19:28-48
and John 2:12-25; 12:12-19

90

Light and dark
John 12:20-50

'I have come into the world as a light, so that no one who believes in me should stay in darkness.'

Who is this Son of Man
To die upon a tree?
Questions since the dawn of time
From those whose eyes don't see.
Incarnate light the love of God
To earthly darkness came;
The voice of heaven as thunder heard
To glorify his name.
The hinge of time is closing
On the Saviour of mankind
As prophecies from ages tell
How faith is hard to find.

91

Stones

Matthew 21:23-46

'... "The stone the builders rejected has become the cornerstone; the Lord has done this, and it is marvellous in our eyes"...'

Matthew 21:42b

Stone-walled vineyard
With stone-faced guardians
Forgetful of the gift
Entrusted to their care,
Pouring forth the grapes of wrath
Upon God's chosen children,
Wrapped in strict observance
Of a stony-heart religion.
Prophets and messengers ignored,
Ostracised and stoned
Until the very Son of God
Himself is killed, disowned.
And so the least shall enter in
By grace and not by law
And they enjoy his vineyard
Both now and evermore.
For the stone that was rejected,
This rock on which we stand,
Becomes the capstone of our faith
To sit at God's right hand.

See also Mark 11:27-12:12 and Luke 20:1-19

92

Choices
Matthew 22:1-14

'So the servants went out into the streets and gathered all the people they could find, the bad as well as the good, and the wedding hall was filled with guests.'

Matthew 22:10

The wedding banquet for the Son,
Ready for the moment
Of his glorious arrival,
But yet no bride is come;
Only guests of honour
Who fail to see the blessings they are given
And so deny themselves
The joys of heaven.
Whilst here amongst the poorest of the poor,
Acceptance of the gift is all,
Refusal still our freedom's choice
But in so doing mankind's fall.
So whilst the schemers try to trap the Son,
God's love remains for everyone
Who gives to him what they could never earn:
The love that they are given in return.

93

Riddles
Matthew 22:15-46

Then the Pharisees went out and laid plans to trap him in his words.

Matthew 22:15

Tricks and riddles set as snares
By zealous men intent on doctrine's triumph
Over grace and love in word and deed,
To catch this Rabbi unawares.
Seven sons, one wife?
Tests of law
And rules for life.
Questions hurled like stones,
First to trap this upstart
And then to take his life.
But Christ has questions of his own,
Not tricks but truth to make God known.
Who is the Christ? Whose is the Son?
And David's prayers from eons gone
Speak wisdom's words
To make men dumb.

See also Mark 12:13-37 and Luke 20:20-44

94

Tombs
Matthew 23:1-39

'Woe to you, blind guides!'

Matthew 23:16a

Walking tombs of dead religion
Press lead-lidded upon a people
Oppressed by empires;
Parched as dry bones by strict observance
Which praises pious practice
But turns blind eyes to cries for mercy,
To strain out gnats from the thin gruel of the law.
Yet through this chosen nation,
Formed in the desert wastes of exile,
Comes the living water of the world's salvation
Clothed in flesh and blood and bone.
The one for whom the tomb itself
Lies dead and buried.
Blessed is he who comes in the name of the Lord.

See also Mark 12:38-40 and Luke 20:45-47

95

Mite
Mark 12:41-44

'They all gave out of their wealth; but she, out of her poverty, put in everything – all she had to live on.'

The love of wealth the root of sin,
But poverty a cross so hard to bear.
Yet always in the history of man
The world divides between the two.
Yet here,
Caught in the light of the Saviour's eye,
A gift transformed by poverty's extreme;
Not just a giving of a single coin
But all that love could muster
And a faith sustain.
True sacrifice
And portent of the greatest gift
So soon to come in blood and pain.

See also Luke 21:1-4

96

End times
Mark 13:1-23

'Do you see all these great buildings?' replied Jesus. 'Not one stone here will be left on another; every one will be thrown down.'

Mark 13:2

At temple's gate,
Built by tyrant's pride
In praise of man,
The coming wrath foretold
In stones that cannot stand.
On a hillside olive grove
End times prophecies
Stir fears and the seeking of signs
Of coming war.
Yet hidden deep within the words
The message of a new beginning,
A crucified king
And a third day's rising.
New life and victory for all mankind.

See also Matthew 24:1-25 and Luke 21:5-24

97

The sign of Noah
Matthew 24:26-51

'Therefore keep watch, because you do not know on what day your Lord will come.'

Matthew 24:42

In Noah's day
The coming flood unknown
Until the first raindrop's fall,
The tears of God are shown.
Hidden in plain sight
Yet there for all to see,
The signs of final ending
In the budding branches of a tree.
This time of second waiting
To watch, to serve and learn,
To share the love of God with all
Until the king's return.

See also Mark 13:24-37 and Luke 21:25-38

98

Three tales end
Matthew 25:1-46

'The King will reply, "Truly I tell you, whatever you did for one of the least of these brothers and sisters of mine, you did for me."'

Matthew 25:40

Three tales tell of his return
And the ending of all things,
Visions of mankind's future
And ways of best preparing.
Faith cannot be earned one for another
Nor given between men;
Each must see
Their own life's need
And the door of heaven open
At his coming.
So, too, each made in his image,
Unique in gift and skills,
To use for pity's sake,
For good and not for ill;
To feed the hungry,
Heal the sick
And help those lost in need.
This is the call, the pilgrim road
And at the end
His good and just reward.

99

Passover's end

Luke 22:7-13

Then came the day of Unleavened Bread on which the Passover Lamb had to be sacrificed.

Luke 22:7

The preparation for the final passover,
Two thousand years of waiting
Coming to fulfilment
In an upper room.
Symbols of salvation
Set upon a table,
Where thirteen men recall
An exodus and new beginning.
Blood splashed on wood,
Unleavened bread
And grapes of wrath
Echo down the ages,
As prayers are offered
And sacrifices made.

See also Matthew 26:17-19 and Mark 14:12-16

100

Servant king

John 13:1-20

'I have set you an example that you should do as I have done for you.'

John 13:15

How could it be that
Kneeling at his followers' feet
The servant king,
Unclothed,
Would stoop to wash away
The dirt and sweat of daily living?
Such humble grace
Lays bare the stain
Of pride ingrained
Beneath the skin
Of mankind's self-sufficiency,
And bids us follow
To the cross
Of selfless giving.

101

Final gathering
Matthew 26:20-35

While they were eating, Jesus took bread, and when he had given thanks, he broke it and gave it to his disciples, saying, 'Take and eat; this is my body.'

Matthew 26:26

Though no-one
Knew that it was so,
The meanings of this final meal
Pass over the heads of his followers
Like angel's wings.
A meal to remember
For two thousand years.
The place of denial,
The bread of life
And cup of forgiveness.
Then stepping out into the night
To weep and pray,
In the midst of a sleeping world,
As the forces of darkness
Gather in the garden
With the kiss of death.

*See also Mark 14:17-31, Luke 22:14-38
and John 13:31-38*

102

Departing words
John 14:1-16:33

'I am the vine; you are the branches. If you remain in me and I in you, you will bear much fruit; apart from me you can do nothing.'

John 15:5

The time is fast approaching
When truth and life will walk the way
Of trial and tribulation
To final victory.
Wisdom's words are whispered
To troubled hearts
That do not see the coming cost,
As vine and branches
Intertwine
And love remains
When all seems lost.
The world of fear and hatred
Gathers in the gloom,
As servant king and followers
Step into dark
Beyond the upper room.
Yet death is but the dawning
Of true life's new rebirth,
One name above all others,
Will overcome the earth.

103

Valediction
John 17:1-26

'Father, I want those you have given me to be with me where I am, and to see my glory, the glory you have given me because you loved me before the creation of the world.'

John 17:24

Eternity itself on the trembling lips
Of the servant Son
Who prays in graced obedience
Across all time,
All space.
To know the one true God
And Christ his only Son,
To see him face to face;
The promise of these final prayers
Spoken in that upper room
For those who heard the words with earthly ears
And those whose lives are yet to come.
Unity in faith and hope
In triune deity,
Prophecies of heaven and earth
And new Jerusalem.
And he who, with the Father
Before the world began,
Knows all things will hold in him,
In Christ the Son of Man.

104

Garden of sorrows

Matthew 26:36-56

He went away a second time and prayed, 'My Father, if it is not possible for this cup to be taken away unless I drink it, may your will be done.'

Matthew 26:42

Whilst followers slumber
In the grip of night,
Face down amidst the olive trees
The Son of God
Sweats bloody drops
Of human terror at
The cup of suffering that
Must be drunk alone.
Torches flicker in the gloom,
As with a kiss, betrayal bites,
Just as Adam in another garden
Eons gone.
Disciples scatter,
Promises unmade,
As scripture is fulfilled
And destiny unfolds.

*See also Mark 14:32-52, Luke 22:39-53
and John 18:1-11*

105

Denial's night

Matthew 26:57-75

Those who had arrested Jesus took him to Caiaphas the high priest, where the teachers of the law and the elders had assembled. But Peter followed him at a distance, right up to the courtyard of the high priest.

Matthew 26:57-58a

In the dead of night
A mockery of justice
Where falsehoods fly
And friendship fails
In the flickering flames
Of a courtyard fire.
One man alone speaks truth,
But visions of heaven
From the Son of God
Bring forth blows
And spit upon his face,
As denial upon denial
Climb upwards
To a cockerel's crow,
To fall in deep despair
And bitter tears.

See also Mark 14:53-72, Luke 22:54-65 and John 18:12-27

106

The innocent I AM
Matthew 27:1-26

*When Judas, who had betrayed him, saw that Jesus was condemned, he was
seized with remorse and returned the thirty pieces of silver to the chief priests
and the elders. 'I have sinned,' he said, 'for I have betrayed innocent blood.'*

Matthew 27:3-4

As innocence is led away to die,
The man of blood-soaked money,
Who cannot see the reason why,
Retreats to hang alone upon a tree
And so, unknown, fulfils
Five-hundred-year-old prophecy.
Coins lie scattered on the temple floor
Where justice fails, and politics and power
Condemn the Christ to cruellest death
And God's great victory.
As Pilate stands to wash his hands,
The mob in blind obedience to Satan's plans
Drives home the punishment of all mankind
Upon the great I AM.

*See also Mark 15:1-15, Luke 22:66-23:25
and John 18:28-19:16*

107

Golgotha's moment
Luke 23:26-43

When they came to the place called the Skull, they crucified him there, along with the criminals – one on his right, the other on his left.

Luke 23:33

Dressed in mockery, crowned in pain,
Anointed with the spit of scorn,
And flayed within
An inch of death,
The Maker of the universe
Endures for pity's sake,
Before the nightmare path
To Golgotha.
There in the place of honour,
At his left and right,
Two sinners
Whose tragedy is bound
Into the passion of the King
And man's unseen redemption.
Soldiers dice with death
Beneath his bleeding feet,
As doubters sneer
And women weep,
And heaven darkens,
Nailed in the hinge of time.

*See also Matthew 27:27-44, Mark 15:16-32
and John 19:17-27*

108

Signs and silence
Matthew 27:45-66

About three in the afternoon Jesus cried out in a loud voice, 'Eli, Eli, lema sabachthani?' (which means 'My God, my God, why have you forsaken me?').

Matthew 27:46

Signs of the time bear witness
To the completion of God's plan,
As words of anguish and despair
Seep from the Son of Man.
And he whose very word
Birthed all of God's creation
Is silent now to drown in sin
For which he is forsaken.
Men from the shadows bear away
His crushed and ruined frame,
And lay him deep in rock-cut tomb
To hide away the shame.
As evening fades to darkness,
Two women sit and stare;
The stone is rolled to seal the door
And silence smothers prayer.

See also Mark 15:33-47, Luke 23:44-56 and John 19:28-42

109

Son rise

Matthew 28:1-15

*After the Sabbath, at dawn on the first day of the week, Mary Magdalene
and the other Mary went to look at the tomb.*

Matthew 28:1

They caught that bright new morning,
Son's splendour rising
And the first rays dawning
Of these latter days;
Where sin is overwhelmed by grace
And death itself has lost its place
Until that final day.
There in the garden weeping
Tears of bitter mourning
And love song's yearning
For the Master's gaze,
His voice breaks through the veil of tears
And grace replaces darkest fears
To sing his highest praise.

See also Mark 16:1-11, Luke 24:1-12 and John 20:1-18

110

New hope
Luke 24:13-35

He said to them, 'How foolish you are, and how slow to believe all that the prophets have spoken! Did not the Messiah have to suffer these things and then enter his glory?'

Luke 24:25-26

Emmaus road,
Slow footfall
Into grief;
Yet conversation
With the Prince of Peace
Unmasks the mystery.
Prophecies and history
Distilled,
Salvation's arc of time
Revealed
In hearts ablaze with new-found hope,
Yet Godhead still concealed.
And so to supper,
Broken bread
New symbol of his covenant;
The risen Christ unveiled.

See also Mark 16:12-13

111

Doubt and faith

John 20:19-31

Jesus came and stood among them and said, 'Peace be with you!' After he said this, he showed them his hands and side. The disciples were overjoyed when they saw the Lord.

John 20:19b-20

Enclosed behind barred doors
And locked in fear of both discovery and death,
Disciples mourn
The ending of salvation's dream.
Then even here
In this place of faltering faith,
Messiah comes
With words of peace and soft command
Borne on the breath of God,
With healing in his wings.
Scarred hands and feet
Bear testimony
To human cruelty and hate,
Now signs of resurrection power
And divine love.
'My Lord, my God,'
Whispered at the Saviour's feet
Echoes through eternity
As faith's encouragement
To all who will believe.

See also Mark 16:14 and Luke 24:36-49

112

Fisher of men

John 21:1-25

The third time he said to him, 'Simon son of John, do you love me?'

John 21:17

Out on the night-time lake
Seven men seek solace and distraction
From the deep;
But none is found,
And in the dawning light
Row home.
There on the shoreline,
A firelight's glow to warm the heart
With fish and bread that mirror miracles
And feed the downcast soul.
Three times asking, three replies,
A trinity of grace and reconciliation
That leads a sinful saint
Once more into his destiny,
And leaves unsaid
A myriad truths
That earth cannot contain
Nor history record.

113

Ending and beginning
Matthew 28:16-20

'And surely I am with you always, to the very end of the age.'

Matthew 28:20b

On a Galilean hillside
That fortieth fateful day,
Eleven faithful followers stand
To hear the Master's
Last command
Before he goes away.
To 'go and make disciples,
Baptise them in the name
Of Father, Son and Spirit
Until I come again.'
Now clustered in that shuttered room,
Bowed down in prayer,
They wait for promised power
They cannot comprehend
And cast by lot Mathias' role
As apostle of God to the earth's end.

See also Mark 16:15-20, Luke 24:50-53 and Acts 1

The Gospels

Matthew

Messiah

Born in David's city
Of David's line,
Fulfilment of ancient promises
Stumbling block divine
To people weary of waiting
Turned inward to proud and pious law
In vain pursuit of 'your way'.
But fulfilment
Lay concealed
In grace,
By which the self-same law
Was made irrelevant
And sin and death disarmed.
From whence
This former tax-collecting follower
Went forth
To bring good news to man.

(From *Start to Finish* by Martin Wild © 2017)

Mark

Servant King

The word passes
First by mouth
And then by hand
As scribe and student follows
Apostolic leaders to heart of empire.
And here
In the sacred city of emperor gods
Servant kingship is proclaimed,
For the son of man came to serve
And give his life as a ransom for many.
Service,
Sacrifice,
Salvation,
Whosoever wants to be first
Must first be slave of all.

(From *Start to Finish* by Martin Wild © 2017)

Luke

Perfection

As his story unfolds,
God as perfect man reveals
His love
For all that he has made.
The Son of Adam
Seeks and saves the lost
Without regard to tribe or tongue
Or life or cost.
Then
Rising from the rocky tomb
To walk and talk,
Emmaus-bound
Till bread is broken once again.
And his witnesses await
The Father's promise
Of power from on high.

(From *Start to Finish* by Martin Wild © 2017)

John

I am love

I AM gave birth to all there is
And all there ever will be,
Word made flesh and blood and bone,
And walked amongst us
With signs and wonders
That all may know
That Jesus is the Son of God.
The word,
The vine,
The lamb,
True bread,
For God so loves us.
The gate,
The light,
The way, the truth, the life,
For God so loves us.

(From *Start to Finish* by Martin Wild © 2017)

Similar Books by the Publisher

A Pocketful of Prayers
Joan Copeland

ISBN 978-1-910197-18-9

This booklet contains 28 prayers in the form of poems that cover aspects of life that we all face – from birthdays to Christmas, from trust to forgiveness, from remembering the past to expectancy of the future.

My Little Book of Bible Quotes
A. Mills-Roberts

ISBN 978-1-907509-69-8

This pocket book of Bible verses is an excellent resource for daily meditation, discipleship and evangelism. Drawn from a range of English translations, these quotes summarize the core Christian message and its relevance to our daily lives.

Books available from all good bookshops and from the publisher:
www.onwardsandupwards.org